Sports Illustrated KIDS

Soccer GOATs

The Greatest Athletes of All Time

BY BRUCE BERGLUND

CAPSTONE PRESS
a capstone imprint

Published by Capstone Press, an imprint of Capstone
1710 Roe Crest Drive, North Mankato, Minnesota 56003
capstonepub.com

Library of Congress Cataloging-in-Publication Data is available on the Library of Congress website.

ISBN: 9781669062929 (hardcover)
ISBN: 9781669063148 (paperback)
ISBN: 9781669062967 (ebook PDF)

Summary: How do you pick soccer's GOATs? Pelé and Marta get a lot of GOAT nods. But is Nadine Angerer the greatest goalkeeper? And what about recent World Cup champion Lionel Messi? It comes down to stats, history, and hunches. Read more about some of the legends of soccer and see if you agree that they're the greatest of all time.

Editorial Credits
Editor: Ericka Smith; Designer: Sarah Bennett; Media Researcher: Svetlana Zhurkin; Production Specialist: Katy LaVigne

Image Credits
Associated Press: Alex Menendez, cover (top left and bottom right), Bippa, 6, dpa/picture-alliance/Carmen Jaspersen, cover (bottom left), File/Carlo Fumagalli, 25 (top), Sipa USA/Pressinphoto/Bagu Blanco, cover (bottom middle); Getty Images: A. Messerschmidt, 27, AFP/Daniel Garcia, 15, AFP/Staff, 21, Al Bello, 23, Archive Photos/Pictorial Parade, 29 (top), Bongarts/Alexander Hassenstein, 17, Bongarts/Christof Koepsel, 7, Bongarts/Lars Baron, 19, Dan Mullan, 4, Feng Li, 26, Hulton Archive/Allsport, 20, Hulton Archive/Evening Standard, 8, Julian Finney, 25 (bottom), Keystone, 22, Martin Rose, 18, picture alliance/Manfred Rehm, 10, Sports Illustrated/George Tiedemann, 29 (bottom), Tom Hauck, 13, ullstein bild/Horstmüller, 11; Shutterstock: Apostle (star background), cover and throughout, Mikolaj Barbanell, 9, ph.FAB, 5, Sunward Art (star confetti), 4 and throughout; Sports Illustrated: Bob Martin, cover (top right), Jerry Cooke, cover (top middle)

Direct Quotations
Page 8, from *Guardian* article, "From the Vault: Remembering the Life and Football of Bobby Moore," theguardian.com
Page 12, from Mar. 16, 2021, *Front Row Soccer* article, "Women's Soccer History Month (Special): What Akers Brings to the USWNT Cannot Be Quantified (1999)," frontrowsoccer.com

All records and statistics in this book are current through 2022.

Printed and bound in China. 6667

Table of Contents

Words in **bold** appear in the glossary.

The World's Game

Whether you call it soccer or football, no other sport is as popular around the world. Over 250 million people play the game—in every country on the planet.

And no other sport **unifies** as many people either. All over the world you will see fans wearing the shirts of their favorite clubs and favorite players.

Kylian Mbappé is still young, but soccer fans already say he will be one of the GOATs. Even though France lost the 2022 World Cup final, Mbappé scored three goals. When France won in 2018, he became only the second teenager to score in a World Cup final—after the great Pelé.

Alexia Putellas is known as La Reina—the Queen—in her hometown of Barcelona. She has led Barcelona to three Women's Champions League titles and has twice won the Women's Ballon d'Or (Golden Ball), an annual award given to the best player in the world. She will play for many more years, but she is already considered one of the GOATs.

With so many players and loyal fans, there are plenty of debates over who the best soccer players in the world are. Soccer's top players are skilled. They're fast. And they're exciting to watch. But only a few stand out as GOATs—the greatest of all time.

Defending Against the Attack

Lev Yashin & Nadine Angerer

The way goalkeepers play today can be traced back to one man—Lev Yashin. Yashin controlled the box like no other goalie before him. He was known as the "Black Spider" for his all-black kit and his diving saves. In his career with the Soviet Union's national team and the Moscow club Dynamo, Yashin kept a **clean sheet** in more than 200 games.

The UEFA European Championship, called the EUROs, is played every four years. Led by Lev Yashin, the Soviet Union won the first tournament in 1960.

Nadine Angerer stopped two penalty kicks in the final of the 2013 UEFA Women's EUROs. She kept a clean sheet against Norway and helped Germany win its eighth European title.

Germany's Nadine Angerer is the only goalkeeper—female or male—to get a clean sheet in every game of a World Cup tournament.

At the 2007 Women's World Cup, she held opponents scoreless in all six matches. In the final against Brazil, she made a diving save to stop a penalty kick by Marta—the top scorer in women's soccer. Germany won the match and later the championship.

Award-Winning Goalkeepers

For a long time, there were two prestigious awards given each year to the best soccer players in the world, both men and women—the Ballon d'Or and the FIFA World Player of the Year. Yashin is the only goalkeeper to ever win the Ballon d'Or. Angerer is the only goalkeeper to win the FIFA Women's World Player of the Year.

Bobby Moore & Lucy Bronze

English center back Bobby Moore had all the skills of a great defender. He made **precise** tackles. He was smooth with the ball when he carried it forward. And he saw the entire **pitch** and **anticipated** what other players would do.

"There should be a law against him," said an opposing manager. "He knows what's happening 20 minutes before everyone else."

Moore (center) was captain of England's team when they won the 1966 World Cup. The tournament was held in England, and it is still the only time England has won the World Cup.

Lucy Bronze (front) played for the English team that won the 2022 Women's EURO tournament. As a member of the French club Olympique Lyons, she won three straight Women's Champions League titles.

Lucy Bronze is also known for her ability to read the game. She gets in position to stop attacking forwards before they get there. And she is especially good in the air, heading passes away from opponents.

As a fullback, Bronze carries the ball up the wing and makes long crossing passes to teammates. She also scores goals, but she likes defending more.

Franz Beckenbauer

Franz Beckenbauer said that the greatest defender ever was Bobby Moore. Most everybody else says that it was Franz Beckenbauer.

Beckenbauer started as a midfielder for Bayern Munich and the German national team in the 1960s. He made long, **pinpoint** passes—a skill he perfected by kicking a ball against the wall of his family's house.

Beckenbauer (left) was the first person to captain teams that won the World Cup, the EUROs, and the Champions League.

By the 1970s, Beckenbauer was starting at center back. But he played in a new way. He set up behind the other defenders to stop anyone who broke through. When he got the ball, he made one of his long, pinpoint passes. Sometimes he carried the ball himself. He invented a new position—the sweeper.

In the Middle of the Action

Michelle Akers

On November 30, 1991, over 63,000 fans filled the stadium in Guangzhou, China. It was the final match of the first Women's World Cup ever.

Forward Michelle Akers scored first for the United States. She hit a leaping header into the net. But Norway quickly evened the score. With two minutes left in the match, Akers broke away on a long pass and scored the winning goal. The United States became the first Women's World Cup champions!

As the team's top scorer, Akers was the first star of women's soccer in the United States. But health problems forced her to move from forward to midfield. "I love dishing and playmaking," Akers said of playing midfield. But she didn't love defending.

Akers worked hard to improve. And she captained the team to a gold medal at the 1996 Olympics and a second World Cup win in 1999.

Akers was a pioneer of women's soccer in the United States. She was one of two women named FIFA Female Player of the Century.

Zinedine Zidane

When teams first put numbers on jerseys, each number represented a player's role on the team. The number 10 was usually given to the team's **playmaker**.

One of the greatest players to wear number 10 was Zinedine Zidane. As an attacking midfielder for Juventus and Real Madrid, he led his clubs to four league titles and a Champions League trophy. He also led the French national team to the World Cup in 1998 and the EURO championship in 2000.

Top Trophy Winners

Only three players have won the World Cup, the EURO tournament, the Champions League, and the Ballon d'Or.

Player	World Cup Team & Year Won	EURO Team & Year Won	Champions League Club & Year(s) Won	Ballon d'Or Award Year(s)
Franz Beckenbauer	West Germany, 1974	West Germany, 1972	Bayern Munich, 1974–1976	1972, 1976
Gerd Müller	West Germany, 1974	West Germany, 1972	Bayern Munich, 1974–1976	1970
Zinedine Zidane	France, 1998	France, 2000	Real Madrid, 2002	1998

Zidane (left) had one of the greatest performances in World Cup history in the 1998 final. Many people expected Brazil to win, but Zidane scored two goals and led France to a 3–0 victory.

Xavi & Andrés Iniesta

During the early 2000s, the most **dynamic** soccer in the world was played in Spain. At the center of it all were two of the greatest midfielders ever—Xavi Hernandez and Andrés Iniesta.

Xavi and Iniesta trained at Barcelona's youth academy. Their model was the senior team's central midfielder, Pep Guardiola. After they reached the senior team and Guardiola became Barcelona's manager, Guardiola built the team around having them play together.

In the seven seasons Xavi and Iniesta were together, Barcelona won five Spanish league titles. They won three Champions League trophies too. And they played together for Spain's national team. During that time, Spain won the EURO in 2008 and 2012 and the World Cup in 2010.

Xavi (left) and Iniesta (right) playing together in a 2007 match against Stuttgart

High-Scoring Forwards

Abby Wambach & Birgit Prinz

The greatest forwards are known for the greatest goals. Two of those great forwards are Abby Wambach and Birgit Prinz.

Abby Wambach scored one of the best goals in the quarterfinals of the 2011 Women's World Cup. The United States trailed Brazil by one goal in extra time. With time running out, Megan Rapinoe kicked a 45-yard cross into the box. Wambach timed her leap perfectly and put an incredible header into the net. The United States went on to win the match.

Abby Wambach

Birgit Prinz

Matching Wambach's scoring pace was Germany's Birgit Prinz. Prinz scored with strong, **accurate** kicks. One of her greatest goals was an **acrobatic** bicycle kick against Argentina in the 2003 Women's World Cup.

Most Women's World Cup Goals

Player	Team	Matches	Goals
Marta	Brazil	23	17
Birgit Prinz	Germany	24	14
Abby Wambach	USA	25	14
Michelle Akers	USA	13	12

Alfredo Di Stéfano

The greatest club in the history of European soccer is Real Madrid. From 1956 to 1960, they won the first five Champions League tournaments. It was called the European Cup then.

Real Madrid's greatest player during that time was Argentine forward Alfredo Di Stéfano. He could defend and attack. He moved everywhere on the pitch. He stopped goals. He set up goals. And he scored goals.

Di Stéfano (center) in a game against Manchester United in 1959

Di Stéfano (left) celebrates winning the European Cup with his teammates in 1959.

Few forwards could score like Di Stéfano. In 11 years with Real Madrid, he scored 308 goals. He finished as the top scorer ever for Europe's top club.

Legends of the Game

Johan Cruyff & Mia Hamm

The greatest players change the game. Two of the most influential players in soccer history were Johan Cruyff and Mia Hamm.

At age 15, Johan Cruyff watched Alfredo Di Stéfano play. He decided that was how he wanted to play, moving freely on the pitch instead of being limited to one position. As a member of the Amsterdam club Ajax and the Dutch national team, Cruyff and his teammates moved from position to position. It was a revolution in how to play soccer.

Cruyff (right) was the first player to win the Ballon d'Or three times. He led his club Ajax to three straight European Cup titles.

One of the players he influenced as a manager was Pep Guardiola. Pep passed what he learned on to Xavi, Iniesta, Lionel Messi, and others.

Mia Hamm changed the idea of who could play soccer. Hamm helped the United States win games during the 1991 and 1999 Women's World Cup tournaments and the 1996 and 2004 Olympics.

Off the pitch, she did interviews and made commercials. This was a time when women's soccer was first gaining attention in the United States. She became the most famous soccer player in the country and inspired millions of girls to start playing.

Hamm (right) is now a co-owner of the Los Angeles Football Club in Major League Soccer. She is also on the board of directors of the Italian club Roma and is a global ambassador for Barcelona.

Lionel Messi & Diego Maradona

No player has won as many trophies as Lionel Messi. In his 17 seasons with Barcelona, the club won the Spanish league 10 times, the Champions League 4 times, and 21 other trophies. Playing for his home country of Argentina, Messi won Olympic gold in 2008 and the South American championship in 2021.

But one trophy escaped him—the World Cup. Some said Messi could not be the GOAT without it. They compared him to Diego Maradona. Like Messi, Maradona was small and quick, an amazing dribbler, and a brilliant scorer. But Maradona led Argentina to a World Cup win in 1986.

In 2022, Messi finally silenced his critics. In the final match of the World Cup, he scored two goals and made his penalty kick. They helped decide the game. Argentina defeated France, and Messi lifted soccer's greatest trophy.

In the quarterfinal of the 1986 World Cup, Diego Maradona scored one of the greatest goals in soccer history. Starting in his own half, Maradona dribbled past five of England's players and scored to put Argentina ahead 2–1.

Messi (center) has also won the Ballon d'Or a record 8 times.

Marta

Some of the greatest athletes are known by one name, like LeBron, Serena, and Michael. The GOAT of women's soccer is known by one name too—Marta.

At age 14, Marta Vieira da Silva rode a bus for three days to try out for a club in Rio de Janeiro. She dribbled past every other player and scored goal after goal. The coaches were amazed. Three years later, she was scoring goals for the Brazilian national team in the Women's World Cup.

Marta has stood above all other women players with her skill on the pitch and her ability to put the ball in the net. And nobody—male or female—has scored as many World Cup goals as Marta.

Marta (10) is the only soccer player to score in five consecutive World Cup tournaments and five consecutive Summer Olympics.

Pelé

One name is above all others in soccer—Pelé.

When he was just 16, Pelé was the top scorer in his professional league. He was quick. And he could control the ball with every part of his foot. Pelé made moves like freestyle tricks, but in the middle of a game.

At age 17, he scored a hat trick in the semifinals of the 1958 World Cup. Then he scored two more goals in the final. For the first time ever, Brazil won the World Cup.

Brazil won again in 1962 and 1970, making Pelé the only player to win the World Cup three times. Meanwhile, his club team, Santos, toured the globe. Pelé became the most famous athlete in the world.

Pelé died on December 29, 2022. It had been 45 years since he played his last match. But Pelé was still one of the most beloved athletes in the world—and he is still known as the GOAT.

Pelé playing for Brazil around 1958

Pelé finished his career playing for the New York Cosmos. His final game was an exhibition between the Cosmos and his old club, Santos, on October 1, 1977. He played for the Cosmos in the first half and Santos in the second half. He scored the final goal of his long career.

Glossary

accurate (AK-yuh-ruht)—able to hit a target

acrobatic (ak-ruh-BAT-ik)—like a move in gymnastics

anticipate (an-TIS-uh-payt)—to expect something to happen before it happens

clean sheet (KLEEN SHEET)—preventing the opposing team from scoring during a game

dynamic (dye-NAM-ik)—having great energy

pinpoint (PIN-point)—very accurate

pitch (PICH)—field

playmaker (PLAY-may-kuhr)—an offensive player who is key to helping a team score

precise (pri-SISSE)—very accurate or exact

unify (YOO-nih-fy)—to bring together as one

Read More

Berglund, Bruce. *Football GOATs: The Greatest Athletes of All Time*. North Mankato, MN: Capstone, 2022.

Borden, Dani. *Soccer's Biggest Rivalries.* North Mankato, MN: Capstone, 2024.

Shaw, Gina. *What Is the Women's World Cup?* New York: Penguin Workshop, 2023.

Internet Sites

FIFA
fifa.com

Olympics
olympics.com

Sports Illustrated Kids: Soccer
sikids.com/tag/soccer

Index

photo by Marta Berglund

About the Author

Bruce Berglund played baseball, hockey, and football as a kid. When he got older, he was a coach and referee. Bruce taught college history for many years. He wrote a history book for adults on world hockey. He is now writing a book about the history of referees and umpires.